God Speaks to Us in
Water Stories

Bible Stories Adapted by
Mary Ann Getty-Sullivan

Illustrated by
Marygrace Dulski Antkowski

Noah and the Ark

Genesis 6:5–9:17

Once there were a man and his wife who pleased God very much. They had a good family and tried very hard to be loving with one another. Eventually their three sons grew up and married three good women. God decided to renew the whole world. So God told the man, Noah, and his wife to build a huge boat, called an Ark.

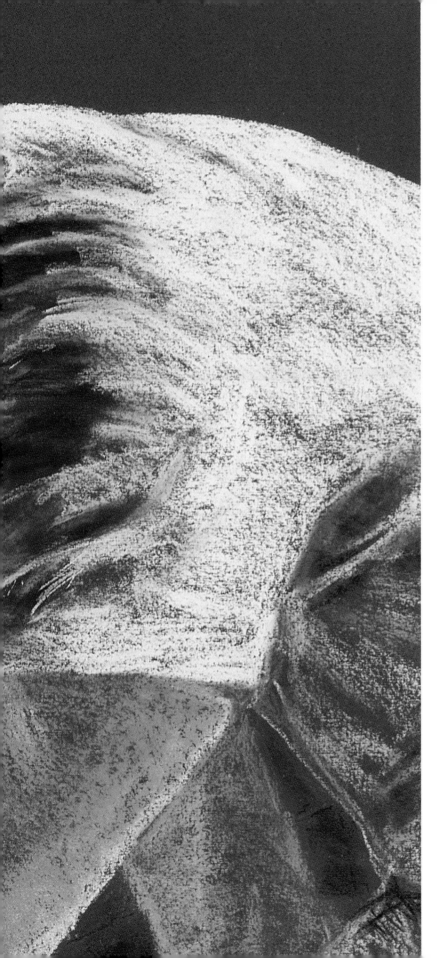

God reminded Noah that this Ark had to be big enough and strong enough to hold one of all the male creatures and one of all the female creatures of the world. God taught Noah what an Ark is and what it is for. And Noah taught these things to his sons. They built the Ark the way God instructed them to. When it was finished, they all set out together on a grand adventure. God would help them prepare so that they would be safe during the time of the recreation of the whole world.

Noah and his family did what God asked. Two of every creature of the world, a male and a female, were given a place on the boat. While Noah and his sons and their sons built the Ark, the women and children gathered two of every living thing on the earth, all the plants and all the animals. Then Noah and his wife, their sons and their wives, and all their family set out with high expectations, trusting in God.

It began to rain. At first it seemed exciting—they watched the rain come down and heard it on the roof of the Ark. It was good to be safe inside the boat with lots of people and animals to play with. But then it kept on raining. And eventually Noah's family became bored; they missed being able to go outside and run free. They also became frightened; they were afraid that everything would be changed when they saw the world again. Noah's family wondered if they would lose everything because it rained for forty days and forty nights.

It rained and it rained. It was a big flood. The water first made puddles and then ponds and lakes; it ran into streams and creeks and rivers. All the seas ran together into one big ocean that covered the whole world. It lifted the big Ark up and up and up. Finally the Ark was sailing high on the waters which had covered the whole world and even the highest hills and mountains. Still the rain continued to fall. Noah's family had to remind each other often that they were doing what God had commanded them to do. So God would take care of them. But it must have seemed sometimes strange and scary for them. And they knew that they had to trust God more every day.

Because it rained for forty days and forty nights, water covered everything. Only the Ark of Noah and his family glided along on top of the water. Finally the rain stopped. But even then, all anyone could see out of the windows of the boat were clouds and sky above and water below. Five months, one hundred fifty days, passed and still there was a lot of water.

After the water rose to its highest point, it began to slowly but surely evaporate. Little by little the boat went down with the water until at last it came to rest on a high mountain named Mount Ararat. Noah knew that they were still very high and that the water still covered most of the land. So he asked everyone to be patient.

Noah then looked for a messenger to send and explore outside to see if they could open the doors of the Ark yet. Noah sent a raven and then a dove out of the Ark. The raven did not return; but the dove came back to the Ark, because it couldn't find a dry place to land. Noah pulled in the dove and waited another seven days before sending the dove out again. This time the dove returned with an olive branch in its beak. Now Noah realized that most of the water was gone and that peace was restored to all the land. Still Noah waited another seven days before he sent the dove out a third time. When the dove did not return, Noah understood that this was a sign that he and his family, his sons and their wives, and all the children could safely leave the Ark.

And now, little by little, there was also sunlight. Then a rainbow appeared that was so beautiful that Noah and his family remembered that they were always in the hands of God. They were very happy. They reminded themselves that God would continue to be with them.

The dove and the olive branch and the rainbow were signs from God who had promised to take care of Noah and his family. And as they left the boat, they knew that God had made a covenant with them and with the new world. God said, "My rainbow is a sign between me and every living creature on the earth. I have made an everlasting covenant with my children and with the earth." And God promised to remember this covenant each time the rainbow appears in the sky. And we should think of that, too. The rainbow means that God is at peace with the whole world. AND SO GOD SPEAKS TO US THIS WATER STORY ABOUT NOAH, HIS FAMILY, AND THE ARK.

The Crossing of the Red Sea

Exodus 1–2; 13–15

God's people lived for a time in Egypt, a strange land for them. They had come to this land many years before, but they were not really at home there. They were forced to work at hard labor, building pyramids for the king of Egypt and even making the bricks out of straw! The king did not even care about their children who were not happy in this strange land.

God wanted the people to go home. And they wanted very badly to go home, too. However, every time they tried to leave, the wicked king stopped them. Time and again the king forbade them to leave because he wanted them to stay and work for him.

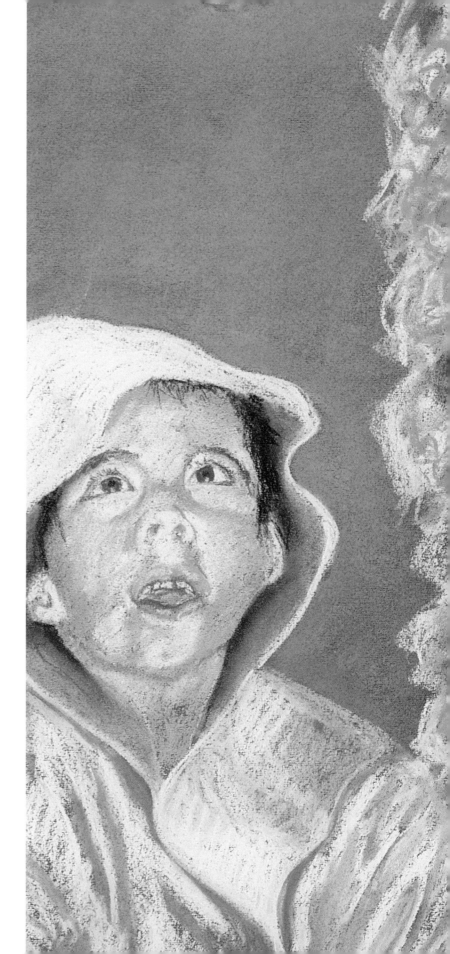

God told Moses to say to the king, "Let my people go." And God told the people not to be afraid. God led them out of the land by a route chosen for them where they would be safe. No one ever saw God, yet the people became aware that God was with them. They learned to trust God, and they began to follow Moses willingly. They started to have hope because they were led out on their journey by a pillar of cloud by day and a pillar of fire by night. The people realized that the cloud and the fire were signs that God was with them. They were amazed that they could travel night and day, twice as far as they had thought. God's presence with them made them much stronger than they were in Egypt, before they knew God by name. In a special way God was now *their* God.

The people were worried and afraid. They were forced to choose between the hard life in Egypt that they had become used to and the promise Moses made to them that was not yet a reality. They knew that if they stayed where they were, they at least had food for themselves and their children.

But they did not know what would happen if they followed Moses. For example, they would have to cross a great water, the Red Sea, in order to finally leave the foreign land and start home. The king first said that they could go, but then he changed his mind. The powerful king followed the people with his great army and tried to force them to return to Egypt.

Out of fear, the people argued with Moses: "We cannot survive. We should never have followed you. Now the king is angrier than ever with us and we will have to return with him and we will be worse off than before." And they asked Moses, "Anyway, how shall we ever cross the sea?"

But God knew what they were thinking and saying. God wondered why the people didn't trust more. The people stopped complaining, however, when they reached the sea. For suddenly the sea opened up before them and the waters formed a wall on both sides, so the people of God could walk across the sea on dry land. When Moses stretched out his hand, as God told him to do, the waters of the sea parted. The same God who made the water and the land, the sun and the moon, now parted the waters so they became like a wall until every Israelite man, woman, and child had passed over and was safe on the other side.

But just as miraculously as the waters had parted to let the Israelites pass over, they now went together and trapped the armies of the king of Egypt. It was chaos for the Egyptians. The water quickly swept them away with the horses and the weapons and all the gear they had brought to enslave the Israelites. At first they had been pleased to think that they had trapped God's people. But the Egyptians themselves got caught up in the high water. God helped the Israelites even though they had not believed. And God continues to help us, promising that if only we believe, we can move waters or mountains. And we will save ourselves a lot of needless worry.

After they had safely crossed over, Moses wanted the people to show their joy to God just as they had shown God how miserable they had been. Moses and all the people broke into a song of thanksgiving for all God had done for them.

Now Moses had a brother named Aaron and a sister named Miriam. Miriam was a prophet, someone chosen by God to speak for God. So Miriam, Moses' sister, took up a tambourine and began to play and dance before God and all the people. The other women joined in song and dance. So did the children. Miriam led the women in celebrating the victory of God over the mean king and his army. The women sang and danced, and everyone had to realize that they had been saved not because they were so strong, but because God is.

Now Miriam's brothers, Moses and Aaron, realized that everyone, even the men, ought to join in praising God's goodness and power. Just as he had led the people through the Red Sea, Moses decided to lead the people in thanking God for their deliverance. Although he himself often felt weak, Moses knew that he had already seen how much God could accomplish through him. So Moses sang, "God is my strength and my courage." And the women sang, "God, in your mercy you are leading us, in your strength you are guiding us." And all the people, women and men and children, joined in singing and praising God and dancing.

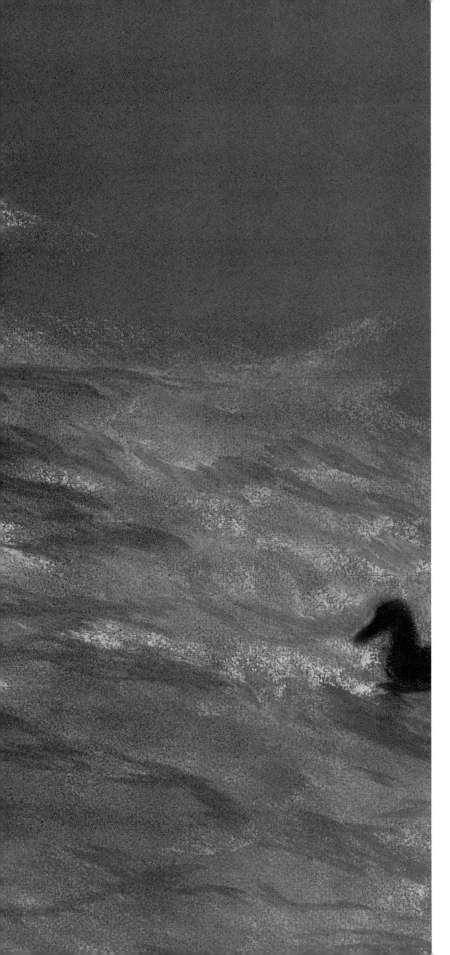

But the people quickly forgot that God could do everything if only they believed. No sooner had they escaped the terrible king than they started again to complain to Moses. This time they complained that, although they had some water, it did not taste very good. It was bitter. Moses knew by this time that God would fix this, too. God told Moses to put some of the wood that lay nearby into the water. When Moses did what God instructed him to do, the water was made fresh and clear and good to drink. And at last the people had nothing to complain about.

God said to them, "Remember, I am your creator and your healer." God can do all things; the only thing people have to do is trust. AND SO GOD SPEAKS TO US THIS WATER STORY ABOUT CROSSING THE RED SEA AND ABOUT HOW THE BITTER WATER BECAME FRESH.

Water Comes out of the Rock

Exodus 17:1-7

Once Moses was leading the people across the desert where it was very dry. The people became very thirsty and started complaining to Moses that God did not seem to care about them. They wanted water so badly. They were hungry, too, and began to be sorry they had ever left Egypt. Because they were unhappy, they changed their view of Egypt and began to think that it was a nice place to be after all.

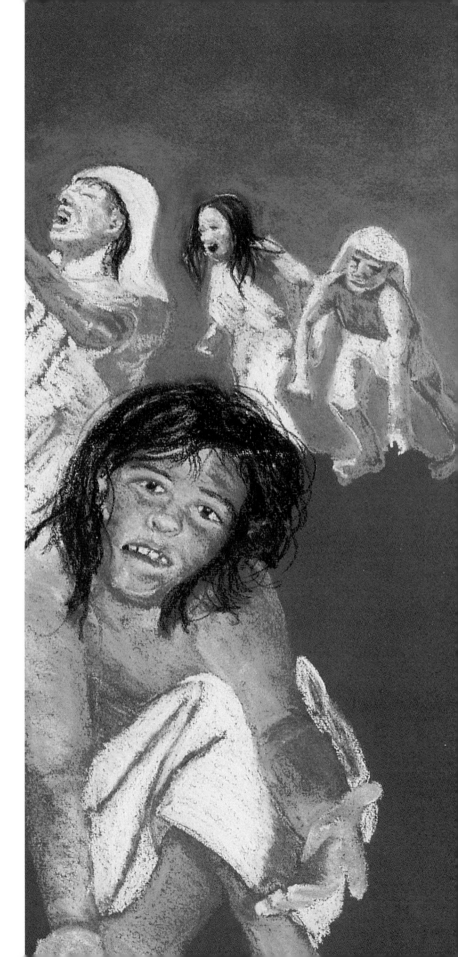

Moses became worried about the people. He wondered how they would ever reach their destination or become a great and holy nation if they were always worrying about the basic things like food and water.

So Moses did what he always did whenever he wasn't sure what to do. Moses prayed. And God listened to Moses and answered him. God told Moses what to do to help the people. "Go to the rock that I will show you. Take your staff and strike it against the rock. You will soon have water for the people if you obey me," God said to Moses.

Moses remembered that it seldom rains in the desert. It seemed strange to believe water would come out of the rock, as God said it would. Moses feared the people would laugh at him for expecting water to come from the rock. He forgot for a moment that God could make water out of nothing at all. But Moses had long ago decided to do whatever God told him to do.

So Moses gathered all the people together. Moses told them that they would receive water which God would give them from a rock. Some of the people did not believe, and they laughed at Moses.

But Moses struck the rock with his staff as God had commanded. And water came out of the rock just as God had spoken and said it would. AND SO GOD SPEAKS TO US THIS WATER STORY ABOUT HOW WATER CAN COME FROM A ROCK WHEN WE HAVE FAITH AND DO AS GOD COMMANDS.

Naaman Is Cured in the Jordan River

2 Kings 5:1-27

Naaman was a good man. He was the army commander of a foreign king. Now Naaman had leprosy, a terrible disease, especially in those days when no one knew how to cure it. In addition, this disease was contagious. This is a disease that caused other people who did not understand to fear being close to Naaman. He, like almost everyone else in those days, thought that illness was always a very bad thing. And he was almost certain he would not live if something could not be done to cure him.

At that time grown-ups hardly ever listened to children, especially girls, and very especially servant girls. But it happened that Naaman had a wonderful wife who had a servant girl with very strong faith. The servant girl (we will call her Mariah) told her mistress one day, "If only your husband would go to my homeland of Israel. There is a man there who is so close to God that God works through him to heal people. He will surely help my master and bring him back to health." The woman told this to her husband, who set out at once with the most hope he had had in a long time.

Naaman did not know Mariah's homeland very well, so he went directly to the king to learn where he might find the holy man who could heal him. But the king had not practiced his religion in a long time. He did not even know that there was a holy man named Elisha who lived in his land. In fact, he thought that Naaman had only come to him to start an argument and perhaps start a war with him. That's how hard it was for him to believe that God would work to cure people.

Now Elisha heard Naaman was searching for him and that the king was afraid of war. So Elisha sent a message saying, "Let Naaman come to me that God may cure him." The king was happy that Elisha was so close to God and would take care of this. And Naaman was pleased to know that he had not made the trip for nothing. Naaman set out with all his men, his fine robes, his horses, and all his chariots and wagons to see the holy man Elisha.

The whole procession went to Elisha's humble house. Elisha was praying when they arrived because he knew that any power to heal had to come from God. So Elisha did not interrupt his prayer with God but sent Naaman this message: "Go wash yourself seven times in the River Jordan and your flesh will be healed. You will be clean and well."

Now Naaman expected something else. He thought that the prophet should have been polite enough to come outside and greet him. He thought Elisha should give him expensive medicines and ask him to do hard things in order to be healed of his terrible illness. Naaman thought that because the disease was terrible, the cure should be hard too. Naaman was not happy that Elisha's instructions were so simple. He said, "Don't we have bigger and better rivers at home where I could wash? Why should I come to this miserable place, and why should I obey someone who doesn't even come out to see me? This man has no manners. I am insulted and I am going home." Naaman was so angry that he thought of fighting Elisha rather than obeying him.

But Naaman had come there with a lot of servants who loved him. Servants, like the little girl Mariah, can sometimes see things even their masters cannot. Although Naaman was a good man, he was also sick, and that made him miserable. So his servants spoke kindly to Naaman. "We have come a long way and we are all hot and tired. Why not go to the river and wash? The water will feel good and cool. If this healer had told you to do something difficult, you would surely do it. But because he told you to do something easy, you have become angry. The water cannot hurt and may help. Please do what Elisha asks."

So Naaman went to the water and washed. The water felt good. He washed seven times. After seven days Naaman was completely healed just as Elisha said. Naaman's leprosy was gone. His hands and arms and feet were perfectly normal and healthy. Naaman returned home to his wife and family a happy man. He was well in soul and body, and now he believed in the God of Elisha, the God of Mariah, the God of Israel. He now knew that this was the true God. He now knew that he was right to obey and not to let his pride get in the way. AND SO GOD SPEAKS TO US THIS WATER STORY OF MERCY AND HEALING.

Baptism of Jesus

Matthew 3:1-17; Mark 1:4-11;
Luke 3:1-22; John 1:1-34

Now for a very long time people
had been hoping that God would
send someone special who would
save them. There came a man who
was quite popular even though he
always told the people the truth
about their sins and about what they
needed to do to change their ways.
When he finished speaking to them,
this man would walk into the water
of the River Jordan and invite people
who believed what he said to come
into the water as a sign of their
belief.

Many people came from all over to be baptized; this man came to be known as John the Baptizer. He said that he was preparing for the coming of the Lord. Even John's clothes and the way he lived in the desert showed that he was very sincere in his belief that the time when God would visit the people was near. John dressed in camel's hair with a leather belt around his waist and only sandals on his feet. He ate the food of the desert—locusts and wild honey and manna—which the people long believed was God's gift to them. John lived like his ancestors the prophets, trusting in God to give him what he needed each day.

By this time Jesus had grown, and he also went from Nazareth to meet John by the Jordan. John recognized Jesus as the very one he had been looking for and preparing for. In fact John thought that Jesus should baptize him rather than the other way around. But Jesus said, "Let it remain like this for now so we fulfill everything God wants of us." So Jesus was baptized along with all the other people who heard John.

And after Jesus came up out of the water, the heavens were opened and the Spirit of God came and rested over Jesus. Some saw the Spirit like a dove and heard the voice of God saying, "This is my beloved child in whom I am well pleased." AND SO GOD SPEAKS TO US THIS WATER STORY OF THE BAPTISM OF JESUS.

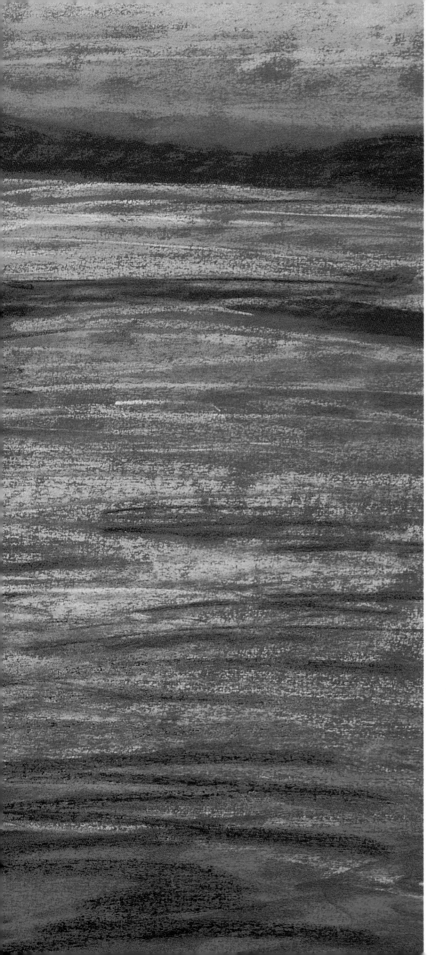

Walking on Water

Mark 6:45-52;
see Matthew 14:22-32;
John 6:15-21

Once Jesus was praying. His friends and a large crowd of people were looking for him because Jesus fed them with loaves and fishes. Jesus got up from prayer and went to his followers. Jesus told them to get into the boat and to cross over to the other side of the lake. But Jesus himself remained behind on the shore.

It was already late at night and beginning to get dark. After a while Jesus wanted to cross the lake, but his disciples had already left and taken the only boat. So Jesus decided to walk out on the water and meet them. It was not an ordinary thing to do, but Jesus had the power of God to walk on water, whereas no ordinary person can do that.

It was not the usual thing to see a person walk on water. The disciples then became very afraid. They did not recognize their friend Jesus. They thought maybe they were seeing a ghost. They were very upset and frightened. They began to pray.

Jesus answered them, "Do not be afraid. It is I, Jesus, your friend." The disciples became calmer when they heard Jesus' voice. But they still did not realize Jesus was coming to meet them because he wanted to be with them. They did not know Jesus could walk across the water. Peter was one who liked to test Jesus. Peter said, "If it is you, Jesus, then say that I can come over to meet you across the water." Jesus said, "Come, Peter, my friend." Peter was very happy, and he started to go to meet Jesus. Suddenly Peter started looking at himself and what he was doing instead of concentrating on Jesus.

As soon as he forgot about who Jesus was, Peter began to sink into the water. But Jesus reached out his hand to Peter and saved him. They both returned to the boat then and to their other friends. After that episode Peter was always ready to remind other people that if they really wanted to reach Jesus and not be afraid, they had to pray and believe. People who concentrate on Jesus and who believe that he is near to help them are saved. We are not alone, and we do not need to be afraid, since Jesus is near. AND SO GOD SPEAKS TO US THIS WATER STORY ABOUT JESUS AND PETER AND HOW THEY WALKED ON WATER.

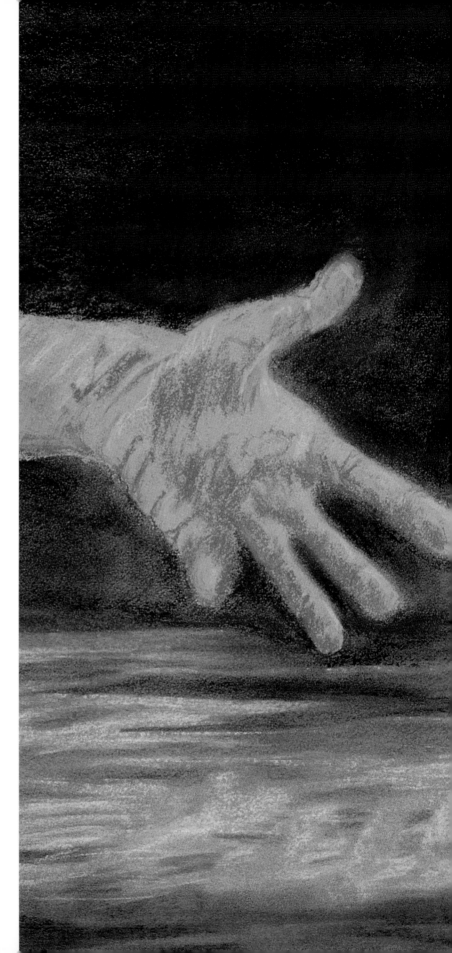

Jesus and the Samaritan Woman

John 4

Once Jesus was traveling in a strange land between his home and Jerusalem, where the Temple was. It is very hot and dusty in that land, and Jesus was thirsty after walking so far. His friends were off looking for food. Jesus sat down beside a well and waited. He hoped that women from the village would be coming along to draw some water for their families. He would ask one of them to give him a drink.

Soon a Samaritan woman came along looking for water for her family. Since Jesus was a stranger, this woman did not expect him to speak to her. You see, Jesus was Jewish, and the Samaritans and the Jews did not get along very well. There were many reasons for this, and after a while people stopped wondering why and just accepted the idea that they should always be strangers. Add to that fact the idea that in those days men usually did not talk to women in the street, not even when they knew each other. Not even if they were married! But Jesus was different. The woman was really surprised when Jesus asked her for a cup of water.

They started talking, and Jesus discovered that the woman had a lot of questions about God and about her religion, about Jesus, about her people, and even about herself. And Jesus talked to her and told her marvelous things. The woman was surprised and excited. She gave Jesus water, but she found that she was the one who was filled.

Later the woman ran home and told all her friends that Jesus was all they had been hoping for. Her friends and, in fact, the whole town ran out to see for themselves. And they believed.

Finally the apostles returned from town. They were amazed that Jesus would speak with a woman because this was so unusual. But they could not deny that the strange woman had done what they were supposed to do. She had shared her water and her story with Jesus. And she had brought all her friends to see him and to believe in him too. AND SO GOD SPEAKS TO US THIS WATER STORY ABOUT THE WOMAN WHO SPREAD THE GOSPEL.

A Liturgical Press Book

THE LITURGICAL PRESS
Collegeville, Minnesota

Printed in the United States of America.

1   2   3   4   5   6   7   8   9

Library of Congress Cataloging-in-Publication Data

Getty, Mary Ann.
     God speaks to us in water stories / Mary Ann Getty.
          p.   cm.
     Summary: Presents Bible stories concerning water, including those
about Noah and the crossing of the Red Sea.
     ISBN 0-8146-2364-6
     1. Bible stories, English—Juvenile literature.   2. Water—
Religious aspects—Christianity—Juvenile literature.   [1. Water—
Religious aspects—Christianity.   2. Bible stories.]   I. Title.
BS551.2.G47   1996
220.9'505—dc20   96-25068
                                                       CIP
                                                       AC